INSIDE TRACK

Author

Gerald Beyersdorff

Photography

Heinz Kluetmeier
Rich Clarkson

Library of Congress Number: 75-1204

ISBN 0-8172-0213-7

Published by **Advanced Learning Concepts, Inc.**
Milwaukee, Wisconsin

A Product of **Advanced Learning Concepts, Inc.**

and Follett Publishing Company
A Division of Follett Corporation
Chicago, Illinois

Contents

1
Tear Into It

The ABC television network had a problem in 1972. ABC had lost the bidding for weekend pro football. They needed something to keep the razor blade and deodorant companies buying commercials on their network. Somebody hit on an idea ... SUPERSTARS! Why not run a competition among the best athletes of every sport?

So down to Florida they went: football, baseball, and basketball stars; boxers, swimmers, and tennis players — and one track man.

The events provided a pretty good test of all-around athletic ability. Among them were a bicycle race, obstacle run, baseball hitting contest, tennis match, a weight lifting event. None of the athletes could compete in their own sport. They had to be good at somebody else's game.

When it was all over, Superstar turned out to be the track man. He was Bob Seagren, Olympic pole vault winner. Reporters and others were surprised that a track man won. They shouldn't have been surprised. Of all athletes, track and field stars are a good bet to be the best.

That's partly because track is the natural sport. We're all born with the basics. We have the ability to run, jump, and throw.

Track and field gives us the chance to find out how good our skills are. How much better than we've ever done before. How we stack up against everyone else.

Back when saber-toothed tigers stalked through the mist, our ancestors jumped gullies, threw stones at their enemies, and sprinted after, or away from, a meal. The good ones made it. Soon they organized games to see just how good they were.

Track requires development of the whole body. It takes physical and mental discipline. And it takes a competitive spirit strong enough to make you do your best even if there's no one but yourself to compete against. Many of the people who might be considered among history's greatest athletes were track stars. There's Jesse Owens, probably the best-known track athlete in history. Herb Elliott, who never lost a race. And Rafer Johnson, who combined speed, strength, and agility to dominate the tough decathlon event in the late 1950s.

Track athletes often move to another sport with ease. Bob Hayes, who was once clocked at 26.9 miles an hour in a 100-yard dash, became an all-pro football wide receiver for the Dallas Cowboys. He was known as the World's Fastest Human. But the New York Giants had a cornerback who could keep up with Hayes. He was Henry Carr, who held world records in both the 200-meter and the 220-yard dashes.

Many people think the top athlete of all time is Wa-Tho-Huck. The great-grandson of Black Hawk, chief of the Sac and Fox, was known as Jim Thorpe because his grandmother (Black Hawk's daughter) married an Irish settler. But his Indian name tells more about his life. Wa-Tho-Huck means "Bright Path."

Thorpe won gold medals in both the pentathlon and decathlon in the 1912 Olympics. In addition, he competed in both the high

and long jumps. A year later, it was found that he had played professional baseball. Because Olympic athletes can't compete professionally in any sport, Thorpe had to give up his medals, records, and the chance to compete in the Olympics again. He then turned professional football player, with such success that sportswriters later named him both Athlete of the Half-Century and Greatest Football Player of the Half-Century. Even with all this, however, Jim Thorpe must take second place to another athlete.

Mildred (Babe) Didrikson Zaharias is the super athlete of all time. Babe got her nickname because she could hit a baseball like Babe Ruth. She could pitch, too, and she spent one season pitching for a men's team.

She excelled at any sport she took up: basketball, golf (she won the National Open three times and the World Championship four), tennis. And track.

It was in a track meet that colorful Babe burst onto the sports scene in 1931. She astounded experts who felt that even the best women athletes were incapable of competing in several events in one day.

Babe won the 80-meter hurdles and long jump that day. And she also set a world record with a 296-foot baseball throw. The next year in a pre-Olympic track and field meet, she won the shot put, baseball throw, javelin throw, long jump, and 80-meter hurdles. And she tied for first in the high jump.

In the 1932 Olympics, she was entered in "only" three events. She set records in the javelin, 80-meter dash, and high jump. She received credit for only two gold medals, however, when judges decided her high jump style was illegal. Babe used the "Western roll." She cleared the bar in a layout on her side.

What made Babe great was the wide range of sports she starred in. And what made her star in so many sports was a combination of

JUNGHANS

her natural ability and something else. That
something else was commitment. She didn't
merely "take up" a sport. She tore into
it with enormous energy. Without commitment, it's hard to get anywhere in athletics.

A listing of track's superstars fails to answer
the question of why we want to run faster,
throw farther, jump higher. The answer: Because it's natural. And the more we find out
just what our natural abilities are and how to
use them, the faster, farther, higher we'll go.

Our competitors are not just those who have
set records in the past. We don't have to
whip everyone to win. We are also competing with ourselves. Our competitors are what
we have been and are now. The winner is
what we can become.

2
Anyone Can Do Something

Take a good look at a track team sometime. The athletes are tall and lean, short and heavily muscled. They're of medium height with big legs, or small legs, or even broomstick legs. Some are broad-shouldered. They look like they've got pads on. And the skinny little kid may not be the equipment manager, but a challenger for the state record for the mile run. They're male and female and they come in all colors.

The variety of events in track and field requires such different talents that almost anyone, with any build, can develop some competence in one.

Most track meets include events in sprints, middle- and long-distance runs, hurdles, and relay races, which are "track" events. Meets often include competition in discus, shot put, javelin, high jump, pole vault, and long jump, which are all "field" events.

The distances for various races are sometimes confusing. That's because the metric system isn't widely used in the United States. The rest of the world uses the system. In the United States, track meets are measured in either yards or meters. The National Collegiate Athletic Association, for example, sanctions some events in yards, such as the 220-yard dash and the 400-yard

low hurdles. It also sanctions events where the distances are measured in meters. Some of those events are the 5000-meter run and the 3000-meter steeplechase. In international competition, such as the Olympics, the metric system is always used.

What's the difference in the length of an event measured in meters and one measured in yards? Take the 100-yard dash and the 100-meter dash. The 100-meter dash is slightly longer than the 100-yard dash. The reason is that a meter is longer than a yard. (A meter is 1.094 yards, to be exact.)

A sprint is any distance up to 440 yards, or 400 meters. A successful sprinter's feet must pound the ground like hail. Arms should pump in time. A simple test determines whether an athlete should work on sprints or go into some other event: the ability to run four-and-a-half steps per second. Technique and training can shave off fractions of a second later, but the four-and-a-half steps per second is the sign of a sprinter. And you're either born with that ability or you're not. It can't be developed. And it has nothing to do with body build.

The middle-distance runner competes in races between 880 yards and six miles. The ideal middle-distance runner has close to a sprinter's speed, plus the endurance of a long-distance competitor. The middle distances require the ability to "coast" at close to full speed and the strength to dash when tired.

The most common middle-distance races in the United States are the mile and the two-mile runs.

Long-distance races are all runs over six miles. Included in long-distance running is the marathon, a foot race of slightly more than twenty-six miles.

Long-distance running requires endurance more than speed. Mental toughness is also required. You must know your own pace and

PORTLAND
BOWLING GREEN
USA
CHICAGO

stick to it. You can't panic if someone takes off and tries to run away from the pack. That runner is probably overexcited and will burn out later.

Among the field events, the discus is the oldest. The discus is a platter-like disk usually made of wood. There is a metal rim around the discus. In the center is a metal plate which controls the weight.

The discus which is used in men's collegiate, national, and international events weighs 2 kilograms (or 4 pounds 6.4 ounces). It is 8⅝ inches in diameter. High school boys usually use a discus that is lighter and smaller than that used by men. The discus used in women's collegiate, national, and international events is even smaller and lighter. High school girls use the same discus as women in their competitions.

All discus throwers must stand inside a circle when they throw. The discus must land within a certain area for the throw to count. Ancient Greek writers claimed that Greek athletes could throw a 12-pound discus 100 feet. There is a reason why the Greeks were never able to throw a discus over that distance. They stood still when they threw. Today's throwers spin their bodies around up to one-and-three-quarters turns before they let go of the discus. This technique puts more force behind the throw.

Discus throwers should have long arms and general body strength, since the act of throwing the discus is a combination of force from nearly every muscle. And the longer the arms, the more force that can be gotten from the spin, before the release.

Putting the shot requires similar body characteristics. Rules say the shot must be pushed rather than thrown. That means an explosion at the final moment.

The shot is a metal ball. In men's international, national, and collegiate competition, the shot weighs 16 pounds. High school

boys use a 12-pound shot. Women and girls usually use a shot weighing 8 pounds 13 ounces.

The javelin throw has carried over from our ancestors' need to throw a spear far and accurately, both in battle and for food. Champion javelin throwers come in all sizes. Coaches claim that having a good long throwing arm and a large hand is helpful. Some experts claim that strength is less important than coordination. They say the slightest change in form will greatly affect distance. In 1964, for example, Mihaela Penes, a Rumanian, broke the Olympic women's javelin record by almost sixteen feet. She never came within two feet of that throw again.

Javelins range in length from 7 feet 2½ inches to 8 feet 6⅜ inches and in weight from 1.327 pounds to 1.761 pounds. At the javelin's center of gravity is a grip, where the athlete holds the spear. All javelins are not designed the same. Some have shafts made of wood, others have metal shafts. The "Western" javelin has a greater total surface area than the older javelins. Wind tunnel tests show that the "Western" javelin goes farther.

In the javelin throw, the athlete first takes hold of the javelin at the grip. The thrower runs full speed to a line which must not be crossed before the javelin is released. When the javelin lands, the point must hit the ground first. If it does not, or if the javelin breaks in mid-air, the throw is no good.

Perhaps no event has had as many different "perfect" styles as the high jump. Arguments over technique have gone on for nearly ninety years. There doesn't even seem to be agreement over the names involved. Techniques have been named for their place of origin (Eastern and Western styles) and for the position of the body at the top of the jump (scissors, straddle roll, layout, belly

roll). And just when they seem to have run
out of names, along comes a record breaker
with another style. Dick Fosbury won the
1972 Olympic high jump by inventing the
"Fosbury Flop." In the Fosbury Flop, jumpers go over the bar headfirst and on their
backs.

Successful high jumpers are tall and leggy.
And they'd better be able to stand the spot-
light. Along with the pole vault, the high
jump is a true glamour event. Success or
failure is as quick as a flashbulb flash. And
there are few more exciting moments in
sports than seeing a jumper sprawled in the
sawdust, watching a wobbling, just-grazed
bar above.

In the high jump, the athlete jumps over a
bar held between two upright poles. Each
jumper decides how many running strides to
use. The angle of approach is also a matter
of individual choice.

The pole vault is nearly as breathtaking for
the vaulter as the spectator. After a number
of precise body motions while clearing the
bar, the vaulter must make sure to push the
pole away — while starting to fall about two
stories.

The pole vault became part of American
track and field in 1850. The pole was solid
and had a spike in one end. The vaulter
would plant the pole into the ground, then
climb the pole hand over hand and drop
over. In 1880, this trick was made illegal.

Poles have been made out of many materials
since then, including bamboo and steel.
Fiberglass is widely used today, because it is
light and very flexible. A pole is chosen according to its weight and where the vaulter
holds the pole while going over. The vaulter
will choose whatever weight pole feels good.

Vaulting champions are not alike in many
ways. They are short and speedy, tall and
muscular, and everywhere in between. But
they are usually well-proportioned. They

USA

need speed for the approach and upper body strength for the lift.

The hurdles and long jump events involve types of sprinting.

Clearing a hurdle has been described as a larger and more artistic sprinter's stride. The height of the hurdle varies according to the event. In the 120-yard high hurdles in National Collegiate Athletic Association meets, the hurdle is 3 feet 6 inches high. In the same event in a high school meet, boys will jump over a hurdle 3 feet 3 inches high. In the 100-meter hurdles in international competition, women clear a hurdle that is 2 feet 9 inches high.

The long jump is simply a leap after about fifteen sprinter's strides. It requires its own techniques, but the first and main requirement is still sprinter's speed.

Relay races are team events. Each runner covers a certain distance, then passes a stick, called a baton, to the next runner. The distance which the runner covers varies. For instance, in meets sponsored by the Association of Intercollegiate Athletics for Women, there is often an 880-yard medley relay. The event involves teams of four women. The first woman on the team will run 220 yards. The next two women run 110 yards each. The last runner covers 440 yards.

From jumping to running, from the hurdles to the marathon, there is something in track for just about everyone.

3
The Long Road

A track meet is the tip of the iceberg. The bulk of the iceberg, the part that doesn't show, is years of training. Sometimes the training pays off in big victories. Sometimes it doesn't. Thousands of athletes suffer hours of punishing training and never become more than also-rans in races that last just ten seconds.

Not all track performers have to be "natural athletes." But it helps. The qualities that make a star are natural to us all. But some people are born with exceptional abilities. That gives them an edge. Especially in sprints.

Right now, there's a little kid running down a sidewalk, through a jungle, along a rice paddy. He turns on full speed, just for the fun of it. He doesn't know it, but his feet are hitting the ground about four-and-a-half times a second. So that makes him a "natural."

But if he's ever going to be a track star, his life will involve coaches, starting blocks, weight training, and practice, practice, practice.

Natural ability carried Jim Thorpe to world fame. He trained only when he felt like it. When he didn't feel like training, he loafed. But there was only one Jim Thorpe. Just

about everybody else has had to make it the hard way. With a lot of sweat and a lot of hurt.

A good example of making it the hard way is Wilma Rudolph. In 1960, Rudolph became the first American woman to win three gold medals in one Olympics. She won in the 100-meter dash, the 200-meter dash, and was on the winning 440-meter relay team. Yet, as a child, she had so many different illnesses that she couldn't even walk until she was eight years old. Training and years of hard work made Wilma Rudolph a champion.

Training means repeating every movement over and over and over again. Then doing it some more. Bobby Morrow, a 100-yard dash star, spent as much time practicing starts as anything else.

Some athletes have special ways of training. Roger Bannister ran to exhaustion on a treadmill every day. Then he went out and broke the four-minute mile.

Spiridon Louis ran beside his mule every day while delivering water. Then he won the 1896 marathon.

Distance runners and marathon runners have special problems they have to train for. Toward the end of the twenty-six-mile marathon, runners sometimes have a less than normal supply of oxygen in their brain. One marathoner tells of hallucinating in the last five miles. He saw ice cream.

Training for distance running can be a drag. Pounding along mile after mile is boring. "Speed-play" training, developed in Sweden during the 1930s, can make a workout more fun. Here's how it works:

1. Run easily for ten minutes to warm up.
2. Pick up your pace and hold it steady for about a mile.
3. Don't stop, but walk rapidly for five minutes.

4. Run easily for sixty yards, then sprint
sixty yards; continue the process until you're
tired.
5. Jog about a mile, taking a half dozen
quick steps now and then.
6. Sprint up a hill, about two hundred yards.
7. On level ground, run fast for one minute.
8. Jog the distance you plan to run competi-
tively (up to one mile).
The exercise should take less than two
hours. It should leave you invigorated rather
than tired.

Even years of practice is not always enough
to make an athlete a success. Athletes must
perfect their technique. Years ago, athletes
could work out their own ideas for cutting
time and gaining inches. In 1900, long
jumper Alvin Kraenzlein worked up a technique that changed his event. Before Kraenzlein, everybody thought the long jump required a high leap from the take-off board.
Kraenzlein decided that speed at take-off
was more important. He tried it out and
broke the world record by three feet.

But athletes seem to have used up their own
ideas for perfecting techniques. Once in a
while, they get help from scientists. For example, one scientist discovered that
strengthening a certain set of arm and
shoulder muscles could cut a fraction of a
second off a sprinter's time. Another scientist found that concentrating on *anticipating*
the sound of the starter's gun means a start
of one-tenth of a second faster than concentrating on the *sound* of the gun. And that's
about a yard at the end of the 100-yard dash.

One thing track athletes have continued to
try to find is a magic diet. Countless athletes
have believed that there must be something
they could eat that would make them a
cinch to win. When the Finns suddenly
showed their heels to other long-distance
runners, everyone started eating black bread
and fish, like the Finns did. Parry O'Brien
had hundreds of other shot putters gagging

on honey before an event. A special 500-calorie meal was once believed to work miracles before a sprint. It was only cereal, toast, butter, sugar, and milk. Scientific tests have proved it a nice breakfast, but that's about all.

Gimmick diets usually lack basic food necessities. Serious athletes should eat sensible, balanced meals. Training and your body will take care of the rest.

4

The Pure Sport

Surely all the years of hard training pay off for the track star. After all, college football and basketball stars sign million-dollar contracts. They become famous and make a lot of money doing commercials. They enjoy profitable professional careers. The track star usually gets...not much.

No college track star is offered a million-dollar contract to turn professional when he or she graduates. A professional track circuit has been organized, but it doesn't draw crowds like the NFL. Doors to success in the business world don't automatically open to former discus throwers. Nor is track a sure road to fame. There's some glory in winning. And some track stars have made a name for themselves. But how many gold medal track winners can you name from the last Olympics?

Not many people have cashed in on track.

The marathon runner who was the hero of Greece in 1896 was offered one wish by the king. He asked only for a cart and a horse. But a few years later, he was sorry that he hadn't asked for more. Very little followed.

After winning four gold medals in the 1936 Olympics, Jesse Owens was snubbed by Adolf Hitler. Hitler refused to attend the awards presentation. Owens also claims that

he never heard a word from his own president, Franklin D. Roosevelt. After the Olympics, the rewards that seemed to lie ahead for Owens faded quickly. For a while he raced against horses for a cut of the gate. Then he went into business. But some people took advantage of him, and the business went bankrupt. Owens' tax problems troubled him for years.

Don Bragg won the gold medal in the pole vault in 1960, but he never reached his real goal: playing Tarzan on TV.

Babe Didrikson won worldwide fame in the 1932 Olympics, but the only money she made from sports came as a professional golfer and baseball player.

Emil Zatopek was a Czechoslovakian national hero in the 1950s. A long-distance runner, he set eighteen world records. In 1968, he publicly supported the ruling government of his country. That government was trying to gain more freedom from Russia. Then Russian tanks and soldiers moved in and threw out the ruling government. Zatopek lost his job, his Communist party membership, his Army position, and most of his pension. He was given a low-paying job under poor conditions, but it was taken away when too many people recognized him and remembered better days. He was given a job where he wouldn't be seen.

Not all stories of track stars end sadly. Ralph Metcalfe and Bob Mathias went from Olympic fame to Congress. Wilt Chamberlain and Bob Hayes used their track skills to make good in high-paying sports: Chamberlain in basketball and Hayes in football.

Track doesn't bring an athlete lots of money. But money isn't the only reward around. For example, if you participate in track, you'll discover that your body is a fine instrument. You will be in shape. And that means more than being able to go up two flights of stairs two at a time without having your heart

pound and your legs feeling like swollen watermelons. You'll also feel more alert, perhaps more confident.

Sometime see if you can catch the look on the faces of runners when they break the tape in a race. It shows a feeling of enough pride, joy, and confidence to take on anything, anyone.

Ask a jumper or vaulter how it feels to look up from the pit and see that the bar is still in place. Ask how it feels to know that the one moment of using every muscle has paid off in clearing a height never before reached.

It's hard to describe the exhilaration of running at top form, coasting along at top speed almost effortlessly. You get the feeling you could go for days, and you're ready to do it. It's like running through the supercharged air immediately before or after a thunderstorm.

Ask a long jumper to describe that moment of flying through the air, knowing that when the jump is over it will be the best one ever.

Or ask a javelin thrower what it's like to watch the javelin soar in a fine arc, farther than it ever did before.

You'll discover that you can improve your own times, your own distances. You'll find that by disciplining yourself, you can push your body toward limits you didn't know you could reach.

You'll find pain and loneliness running up and down hills. And you'll know boredom, bursting out of the blocks time after time. But suddenly you're in a meet, scoring points for yourself and your team; and the next week, the hills seem flatter and the blocks more comfortable. You've done it all by yourself. You've beaten weakness and found strength.

True, you can't take those feelings to the bank and deposit them. But they add up to something better.

5
The Big Show

This tale of how the Olympics got started may not be true. But the ancient Greeks told it anyway.

A certain King Enomaus ruled Olympia, on the plains below Mount Olympus. The king had a daughter, Hippodamia. Hippodamia had so many suitors her dad set up a game to decide which one was good enough to marry her.

It was a simple game. And it was a silly game. The boy friends would grab Hippodamia and try to escape in a chariot. If Dad didn't catch them, they could be married. Of course Dad had the fastest horses in the kingdom, so the first thirteen times the game was played he won. The losers were killed.

Number Fourteen was a brave lad named Pelops. He was also tricky, and he bribed King Enomaus' charioteer. The race began. Pelops grabbed Hippodamia and took off with the king not far behind. The king was closing in when, thanks to the work of the charioteer, an axle broke. So did the king's neck.

To celebrate his double victory of gaining a bride and getting rid of a nasty father-in-law, Pelops set up the games and religious rites

that turned out to be the first type of Olympic event.

That story, true or not, was a good start for the many Olympic stories that followed.

The Olympic games started about 776 B.C. These early games were sort of a substitute for war, with the best runners of one city racing the best of another. Soon, however, the games became a sport for playboys. That's because the rules said that only freeborn Greek men who swore that they had trained for at least ten months could compete. That left out everyone but rich Greek males who lied about how much they trained.

By the time the Romans conquered Greece, the Olympics included competition in choral music, dancing, and an event called the pancration. Despite its fancy name the pancration was nothing more than a street fight.

Eye gouging, hitting below the belt, and strangling were common in the pancration. No holds or blows were barred. The event was decided when one fighter raised his hand in surrender.

In one pancration, an athlete named Arrachion was viciously twisting his opponent's leg while the opponent was busily strangling Arrachion. Arrachion gave the leg one last twist as he himself died of strangulation. But the leg pain was too much. At the moment of Arrachion's death, his opponent raised his hand in surrender. The dead body of Arrachion was declared the winner.

The Romans continued the Olympic games until Emperor Theodosius stopped them in A.D. 394. A Frenchman brought the games back to life in 1896, and it was decided that the best place to hold them would be near their birthplace, in Athens, Greece.

Going into the last day of those first "mod-

ern'' Olympics, not one event had been won by a Greek.

The last event in 1896 was the marathon. The event was named after the Battle of Marathon in ancient Greece. In that battle, the army of the city of Athens fought the army of Persia. If the Persians had won, they would have marched on Athens and killed the Athenians. But against great odds, the Athenians defeated the Persians. And a messenger named Pheidippides ran more than twenty-six miles to tell the people of Athens they were safe. He delivered his message — ''We won!''

Then he dropped dead.

Spiridon Louis knew the story of Pheidippides. Spiridon was a Greek shepherd and water carrier who had read about the Olympics returning to Greece in 1896. He considered it his sacred duty to compete. So he entered the marathon, which turned out to be almost the same route Pheidippides had run twenty-four centuries before.

A deeply religious man, Spiridon prayed and went without food the day before the race. Now that's not the usual way to warm up for a long-distance race. By starting time, he had an empty stomach and a weakened body. But no matter. He won the race by seven minutes over his nearest competitor. Spiridon became an instant national hero. He received free clothes and meals, free haircuts for life, and a free horse and cart.

The 1896 games were the first modern Olympics. And yet, while each Olympiad since then has become more modern in some ways, with new events, better TV coverage, and more comfortable facilities, each Olympic keeps one foot firmly planted in history.

Pageantry is a big part of the Olympics. The flame that burns during the games is lit from the ''eternal'' flame that burns in Greece. Runners carry a torch in relays to the

USA
DDR

games, which are held every four years.

The Olympics are for amateurs. Many countries, however, pay their athletes' "expenses" or give them easy, high-paying jobs so they can afford to compete. Officially, the games are contests between individuals or teams. But newspapers all over the world like to write about which country is leading.

And, because the Olympics hold the attention of the world every four years, they have sometimes become a target for political acts that have nothing to do with sport. Some people have had messages they wanted to give the world. So they used the Olympics to do it. In 1908, the English Olympic Committee wanted to show the world what they thought of the American committee. So they didn't fly the American flag with all the other flags around the stadium. And they planned events on a Sunday, knowing that many on the American committee and team believed there should be no sports on that day.

In 1968, the message of two American sprinters at the Olympics was against racial discrimination. Tommie Smith won the 200-meter run. The U.S. national anthem was played in honor of Smith's victory. As the music played, Smith and teammate John Carlos, who finished third, bowed their heads and raised black-gloved fists in the "black power" salute.

In 1972, a group of Arabs raided the Olympic Village, where Israeli and other athletes were staying. Two Israelis were killed in the Olympic Village. Then the drama moved to Fuerstenfeldbruck Air Base. There the Arabs expected to board a plane with the eleven Israelis they had brought with them from the Olympic Village. The Arabs wanted the plane to fly to Cairo. But police opened fire. Two Arabs were killed. A third jumped from the helicopter in which he and some of the Israelis had been flown to the air base. He threw a grenade into the helicopter. Other Arabs started shooting.

When it was all over, seventeen people had been killed: eleven Israelis, five Arabs, and one policeman.

There were over six thousand newspaper and television people on the scene. People all over the world soon learned of the tragedy. The Arabs were using the Olympics to focus the attention of millions on their hatred of the Israelis. Most people in the world were horrified by their actions. Willie White, an American long jumper, said, "They're all part of our family — the family of man. It's horrible." Many people felt that way.

Protest was on everyone's mind that year. So after Dave Wottle won the 800-meter race, people thought he was protesting too. Wottle was wearing a cap to keep his hair out of his eyes. In the excitement, he forgot to take the cap off when he was given his gold medal and the U.S. national anthem was played. "Another protest!" some people complained.

Wottle had to put up with dozens of interviews explaining it was just a mistake.

The Olympics have seen some good times... and some rough moments. But despite all the other things that creep into the Olympic games, and all the disagreement over the judges' decisions, the Olympics still bring together many of the best athletes from all over the world. And that's what they're supposed to do.

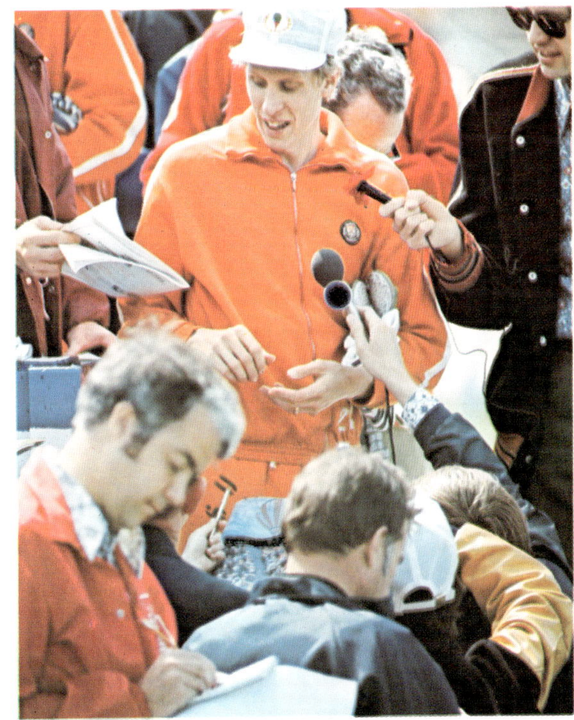

6
A Special Victory

If there is one thread that ties the Olympics together it's this: They bring out either the best or the worst in athletes. That's because the Olympics are the test of who is best in the world. They're bigger than the Super Bowl and the World Series together. It takes a big performance to win. So big, some athletes are overwhelmed by it all and blow the biggest event of their lives. So big, others hit a peak never reached before or after.

Jim Ryun ran in his first Olympics when he was seventeen. He surprised the experts by making it all the way to the semi-finals before failing to qualify. He came back to the U.S. with great publicity, and by the next Olympics, he had broken the world records in the 800-meter, 1500-meter, and mile runs.

Ryun missed much of the 1968 season because he was sick. He barely recovered in time to make the U.S. team as a 1500-meter runner. A sentimental favorite of many, Ryun took second to Kip Keino of Kenya at the games. Many thought Ryun was one of the team's biggest failures. Experts now say that his winning a silver medal was remarkable.

Ryun himself was upset, and he quit running a year later. But in 1972, he decided to take one last crack at an Olympic gold medal. He tried training in Kansas, in California, in

KANSAS
TRACK
100

USA
K.S.U.
TRACK

Oregon, and back in Kansas again. He switched coaches. He ran on hills and flat land. He went to doctors for his allergies. But he continued to run a 3:53 mile in one meet and a 4:19 mile in the next.

He went to the 1972 Olympics as a sentimental favorite again, hoping for victory. While trying to qualify, he tripped, or was tripped, and never even got to try for the big one.

Michel Jazy, a Frenchman, was Europe's best distance runner in the late 1950s and early 1960s. He had set several world records in non-Olympic races. He had entered the Olympics in 1956 and 1960, but he had only a second place to show for it. He entered the Olympics again in 1964, to prove that Europe had the best 1500- and 5000-meter runners in the world.

In the 5000-meter finals, Jazy was running the race he wanted. In the middle of the last lap, he passed Australia's Ron Clarke and seemed ready to capture that first gold medal.

But suddenly, on the backstretch, Bob Schul challenged him. Unprepared for the American, Jazy lost his cool and Schul surged ahead. At that important moment, Michel Jazy found it impossible to meet the challenge.

He fell back to second, third, and finally fourth place. And when the 1500-meter event came, Jazy's collapse was complete. He didn't even qualify for the finals.

In later years, he would again run well. But in the one instant where Olympic champions are formed, Michel Jazy fell short.

Betty Cuthbert was barely eighteen when the 1956 Olympics came to Australia. She had won the Australian title in the 220-yard dash that year, but was certainly no proven star.

Besides, she was under the pressure of running in three events — the 100 and 200 meters, and the 400-meter relays. An Australian

1008

sportswriter called her just a "lissome lass."

She tied the Olympic record in the 100 meters and the world record in the 200 meters for two gold medals. And she ran a perfect anchor leg in the relays for a new world record and her third medal.

Betty Cuthbert went on to set a total of sixteen world records in every distance from 100 to 440 yards. She was injured in 1960 and missed the Olympics that year. She retired for a while, then decided to try for a comeback in 1964. She took another gold medal that year, with a record in the 400 meters. Just a "lissome lass." Hah! Better running than most.

Lutz Long was a German long jumper in the early days of Hitler's power. As the pride of Nazi Germany, it was up to Long to stop the gold that American Jesse Owens was piling up in the 1936 Olympics in Berlin, Germany.

Long's plan had always been to scare his opponents early. So in qualifying to see who would make the finals, Long always went for a super jump right away. That day in 1936, it worked. Long got off a tremendous jump. Owens had three chances to qualify. The first time, he tried extra hard to match Long's jump. He fouled.

On his second try, Owens was too careful because of the foul. So he got off a poor jump.

Only one chance left for Owens to qualify.

Lutz Long and the 110,000 fans in Berlin could see that Jesse Owens was upset. He seemed a sure bet to fail. The gold medal was as good as in Long's pocket. All he had to do was watch.

But Long took to heart all the sayings about the Olympics having to do with brotherhood and goodwill. He took Owens aside before his final jump. He calmed him down and offered an idea that might help him. On his third and last chance, Owens qualified.

That meant Owens would be jumping
against Long in the finals. In the finals, Long
broke the Olympic record. But so did
Owens. By more. And when it was over, Lutz
Long took the man who had beaten him and
led him around the stadium to accept the
cheers of the German crowd.

Five years later, Germany and the United
States were at war with each other.

But Lutz Long and Jesse Owens had become great friends. They wrote to each
other often, even during the war. Lutz Long
died in World War II, and is buried some-
where in an African desert. Jesse Owens has
the gold medal Long could have won. But
Lutz Long won his own kind of Olympic victory.

A victory in the spirit of the Olympics — and
of all sport.

Pre-Reading Aids

1
Tear Into It

Purpose for Reading

Who is the super athlete of all time?

Why do athletes enjoy track and field?

The answers to these questions can be found in Chapter 1.

Important Vocabulary

The following words may be of help as you read Chapter 1:

discipline (dis ci pline; dis′ə plin), *n.*
training, control

He had great physical *discipline* and could do things most athletes could not.

competitive (com pet i tive; kəm pet′ə tiv), *adj.*
able and willing to make the effort required to get something wanted by others

Ruth is a *competitive* person; she'll be able to stand the pressure and end up winning.

agility (a gil i ty; ə jil′ə tē), *n.*
the ability to move quickly and easily

He climbed the tree with the *agility* of a monkey.

excelled (ex celled; ek seld′), *v.*
did better than, outdid

Dan was not good at most sports, but he *excelled* at wrestling.

astounded (as tound ed, ə stound′əd), *v.*
greatly surprised, amazed

Many tennis fans were *astounded* when Billie Jean King beat Bobby Riggs so easily.

commitment (com mit ment; kə mit′mənt), *n.*
complete involvement or giving of oneself

His high grades are the result of a *commitment* he made to doing well.

Pre-Reading Aids

2

Anyone Can Do Something

Purpose for Reading

What events make up a track meet?
What does it take to perform them well?

You'll learn the answers as you read Chapter 2.

Important Vocabulary

You may find the following words helpful as you read this chapter:

competence (com pe tence; kom′pə tənz), *n.*
ability, able to do something well

Everyone thought the guide had the *competence* to lead them out of the forest safely.

sanctions (sanc tions; sangk′shənz), *v.*
sponsors, gives approval or permission

The local committee *sanctions* all the tennis matches held each summer in the neighborhood park.

technique (tech nique; tek nēk′), *n.*
a special way of doing something

Many painters develop their own special *technique*—a style different from anyone else's.

endurance (en dur ance; en dür′əns), *n.*
the power to last or keep on

Lisa must have great *endurance* because she jogs ten miles every day.

coordination (co or di na tion; kō ôr də nā′shən), *n.*
two or more things working well together

Good physical *coordination* is important in order to do well in most sports.

precise (pre cise; pri sīs′), *adj.*
exact or careful

The hunters took slow, *precise* steps on the ice.

well-proportioned (well pro por tioned; wel′prə pôr′shənd),
adj.

having a good, balanced shape

One of the reasons he starred in swimming was because he had such *well-proportioned* shoulders and arms.

Pre-Reading Aids

3
The Long Road

Purpose for Reading

How do track and field stars train?
What besides practice do they need?

You'll find the answers to these questions in Chapter 3.

Important Vocabulary

You may find these words helpful as you read Chapter 3:

exceptional (ex cep tion al; ek sep′shə nəl), *adj.*
unusual, uncommon

Darrell did an *exceptional* job and was rewarded for all he
had done.

exhaustion (ex haus tion; eg zôs′chən), *n.*
tired, completely worn out

They were in a state of total *exhaustion* after staying up all
night to finish the project.

hallucinating (hal lu ci nat ing; hə lü′sə nā ting), *n.*
seeing or hearing imaginary things

Hallucinating is not unusual for some people if they are left
alone for long periods of time.

invigorated (in vig or at ed; in vig′ə rā təd), *adv.*
full of energy or strength

They felt *invigorated* by an early breakfast and a swim in the
lake.

anticipating (an ti ci pa ting; an tis ə pā′ting), *v.*
looking forward to

The salespeople reported to work early because they were
anticipating a huge crowd for the Christmas sale.

4

The Pure Sport

Purpose for Reading

What does a track star gain from the hard work required to win?

You'll find the answers in this chapter.

Important Vocabulary

These words may be of help as you read:

profitable (prof it a ble; prof′ə tə bəl), *adj.*
useful, financially beneficial

The garage sale held by the neighborhood was very *profitable.*

participate (par tic i pate; par tis′ə pāt), *v.*
to take part in, to be involved in

The students who *participate* in the music contest will be allowed to miss a day of school.

confident (con fi dent; kon′fə dənt), *adj.*
certain or sure

Lynne was *confident* that she would be chosen for the baseball team.

exhilaration (ex hil a ra tion; eg zil ə rā′shən), *n.*
high spirits

The team's *exhilaration* after winning was in sharp contrast to the fear and worry they had felt before the game.

effortlessly (ef fort less ly; ef′fərt ləs lē), *adv.*
easily, requiring no work

The eagles seemed to soar through the air *effortlessly.*

Pre-Reading Aids

5
The Big Show

Purpose for Reading

What are the Olympics?
How have they changed?

Important Vocabulary

chariot (char i ot; char′ē ət), *n.*
two-wheeled vehicle pulled by horses, used in ancient times in races

The driver of a *chariot* had to be strong to control the high-strung, nervous horses.

freeborn (free born; frē′bôrn), *adj.*
not born as a slave

In that country, all *freeborn* people could vote; slaves were not allowed to.

gouging (goug ing; gou′jing), *n.*
forcing out, digging out

Gouging an eye is not a big problem in sports today, thanks to special safety equipment.

viciously (vi cious ly; vish′əs lē), *adv.*
wickedly, with evil intentions

Charles pinched his sister *viciously* when their father was not watching.

facilities (fa cil i ties; fə sil′ə tēz), *n.*
buildings which serve a special purpose

The new high school had some of the best sports *facilities* in the city.

pageantry (pag eant ry; paj′ən trē), *n.*
a splendid show, a gorgeous display

Millions of people watched the *pageantry* of the Thanksgiving Day parade on television.

discrimination (dis crim i na tion; dis krim ə nā′shən), *n.*
making a difference in favor or against something or someone.

Racial *discrimination* in hiring is against the law.

Pre-Reading Aids

6
A Special Victory

Purpose for Reading

What is special about the Olympic games?

You'll find the answer as you read this chapter.

Important Vocabulary

These words may be of help as you read:

overwhelmed (o ver whelmed; o vər hwelmd′), *v.*
completely overcome

Paco was *overwhelmed* when he saw how much bigger his opponent was.

publicity (pub lic i ty; pub lis′ə tē), *n.*
information designed to attract people's interest and attention

The shooting received so much *publicity* in the newspapers that a fair trial would be impossible.

sentimental (sen ti men tal; sen tə men′təl), *adj.*
having warm or tender feelings

When Ms. Newmark unpacked the trunk in the attic, she found many *sentimental* letters she had kept over the years.

remarkable (re mark a ble; ri mar′kə bəl), *adj.*
amazing, unusual

Richard made a *remarkable* recovery from the accident.

qualify (qual i fy; kwol′ə fī), *v.*
to gain the right to compete in an event

She can *qualify* for the race only if she can drive fast enough in the time trials.

Discussion Questions

Chapter 1

Who is the greatest athlete on the sports scene today?

In what ways is he or she like Babe Didrikson Zaharias?

If you wanted to persuade the school board of a nearby town to add track and field to their athletic program, what would you say?

Chapter 2

Which events in a track and field meet seem to you to depend *most* on natural ability?

Which seem most difficult? Why?

Chapter 3

If you were coaching a track team, would you stress practice or technique? Why?

Chapter 4

You're a coach and want to persuade young people to go out for track rather than tennis or baseball. What will your arguments be?

Chapter 5

If you were asked to list the major arguments for and against continuing the Olympics, what arguments would you select?

What is your own point of view about continuing the Olympics?

Chapter 6

Attack or defend the idea that the Olympics do not provide a fair test of how good an athlete is.

Would you agree or disagree with the statement that Lutz Long is the real super athlete of all time? Why?

Related Activities

If you want to learn more about track and field, you may want to do one or more of the following:

1. Interview several members of a track team. Try to find out what it is about the sport that appeals to them. Record your interview on tape or in written form. Edit your material and present it to your class. Or, submit it to your school or local newspaper for publication.

2. Try a track or field event you've never competed in. Try it several times. Record your impressions in words, in pictures, in sound, or in some other form. Report what your feelings are to your class.

3. Visit your school or public library. Find out what resources are available in the area of track and field. List these and describe each one briefly. Post your list in your classroom.

4. Write several jokes about track and field—or locate some in the newspaper or in magazines. Post these where they can be enjoyed by others in your class.

5. Make a detailed drawing of an Olympic gold metal. Try to learn who designed the medal and what the figures on the medal represent. Display your drawing in your classroom and report your findings in any way you choose.

6. Attend one or more track meets and carefully watch an event that you find interesting. Try to capture the feelings of that event in words, in pictures, in sound, or in some other way. Present your impressions to your classmates.

7. Create some cartoons, or make one or more comic strips about track and field. Post these on the bulletin board.

8. Borrow a discus, a shot, a hurdle, or some other pieces of equipment from a track team. Explain these to your class. Display them for others to see.

9. Make a list of little-known facts about track and field. You may want to include some or all of the following:
   phony finishers in the marathon
   the identity of the man and woman who won the most

individual gold medals in the Olympic games
the speed reached by the fastest woman runner of all time
other facts of interest to you
You may want to ask your librarian for assistance in finding the information.

10. On a map of the United States, label the locations of the summer Olympics from 1912 to the present. Indicate the dates of the games. For each location, indicate the number of Olympic and/or world records in track and field that were broken during the games.

11. Time your friends or the sprinters on several track teams as they race for a distance of fifty or more yards. How many steps per second does each runner take? Record your findings and report your research to your class. What conclusions do you draw?

12. Select a track or field event that especially interests you. Determine the time, height, or distance of the winning men's or women's Olympic performances since 1936. Make a graph or some other visual aid that summarizes these. Present your findings, including your visual aid, to your class in oral or written form.

13. Visit your school or local library. See what resources are available that describe the Jesse Owens-Lutz Long incident in detail. Read one or several of these and report on your readings in a form that you and your teacher agree upon. If few or no sources are available, ask the librarian for help in determining what might be purchased. If possible, help the librarian in ordering one or more of these.

14. Make a collage or mobile reflecting your impressions of one or more track and field events.

15. Make a list of present world records in major events of men's and women's track and field. For comparison, make a list of world records in the same events of at least thirty years ago. Report your conclusions in oral or written form.

16. Attend two or more practices of a track team. Pay particular attention to the events that most interest you. Talk to the athletes. Try to learn why they practice the way they do. Report your findings to your class.

17. Compile a list of words that reflects the sights and sounds of the various events of track and field. Create a card game from these. Or create another kind of game that is of greater interest to you.

18. Read one or more sources about Jim Thorpe or Babe Didrikson Zaharias—or about another track star who interests you. Try to get a feeling for the kind of person he or she was or is. Make a brief report—oral, written, or in some other form—available to your classmates.

19. Compare present U.S. records to present world records in several track or field events. What conclusions do you draw? Summarize these and make them available to your classmates.

20. Make a photo journal of the practices, the meets, the successes, and the defeats of one or more members of a track team. Try to focus on the hard work, the joy, or whatever seems most important to you. Display your journal in your classroom.

<table>
<tr><td>Reading and Curriculum Editor</td><td>Peter Sanders, PhD.
Wayne State University</td></tr>
<tr><td>Associate Reading Consultants</td><td>John Clark, M.A.
Cincinnati Public Schools
Cincinnati, Ohio

Edward Daughtrey, M.S.
Norfolk City Schools
Norfolk, Virginia</td></tr>
<tr><td>Story Editor</td><td>Patrick Reardon</td></tr>
<tr><td>Associate Editor</td><td>Deborah Gardner</td></tr>
<tr><td>Coordinator of Learner Verification</td><td>Peter Sanders, PhD.</td></tr>
<tr><td>Related Activities and Vocabulary Sections</td><td>Peter Sanders, PhD.</td></tr>
<tr><td>Photography Editor</td><td>Eric Bartelt</td></tr>
<tr><td>Graphic Design</td><td>Interface Design Group, Inc.</td></tr>
<tr><td>Color Process</td><td>American Color Systems</td></tr>
<tr><td>Lithography</td><td>A. Hoen & Co.</td></tr>
<tr><td>Binding</td><td>Lake Book Bindery</td></tr>
</table>

Manufactured in the United States of America to Class A specifications of The Book Manufacturers' Institute

2 3 4 5 6 7 8 9 0   80 79 78 77 76